Gray's *Venison* Cookbook

A MENU COOKBOOK

Also by Rebecca Gray

American Artisanal:
Finding the Country's Best Real Food, from Cheese to Chocolate

Chefs Go Wild:
The Best Fish and Game Recipes on the Planet

Eat Like a Wild Man:
110 Years of Great Game and Fish Recipes

The New Gray's Fish Cookbook:
A Menu Cookbook

The New Gray's Wild Game Cookbook:
A Menu Cookbook

Venison

When Fishermen Cook Fish

As contributing editor:

Joy of Cooking:
75th Anniversary Edition

Gray's Venison *Cookbook*

A MENU COOKBOOK

Rebecca Gray

GRAYBOOKS
LYME, NEW HAMPSHIRE

Text Copyright © 2010 Rebecca Gray
Illustrations Copyright © 2010 DeCourcy Taylor Jr.
All rights reserved.

ISBN-10: 1-935655-20-5
ISBN-13: 978-1-935655-20-6

Published by
GrayBooks LLC
1 Main Street
Lyme, New Hampshire 03768
www.GraybooksPublishers.com

First Edition
Softcover

Printed in The Unites States of America
on acid-free paper.

For the deer hunters, and all the venison eaters, in my family

Contents

Venison 11

Venison Black Bean Chili — 16
   Baby Spinach and Arugula Salad with Avocado and Egg
   Fennel Seed Bread
   Ginger Angel Crisps

Venison Burgers with Chateaubriand Butter — 22
   Fried Bread
   Vegetable Salad
   Fresh Fruit

Saddle of Venison — 26
   Potatoes and Porcini
   Braised Fennel
   Clafoutis

Venison Strip Steaks — 31
   Fried Potato Skins
   Grilled Red Pepper Salad
   Strawberry Ice Cream

Venison Stew — 37
   Homemade Pasta
   Crusted Blueberry and Cream Cake

Venison Stew with Artichoke Hearts and Sun-dried Tomatoes — 42
   Basil Bread
   Green Salad
   Custard Oranges

Venison with Port — 47
   Roast Potatoes
   Sautéed Watercress
   Meyer Lemon Sherbet

Venison Scallops   50
    Persillade Potatoes
    Green Beans
    Tarte Tatin

Venison Chops with Pignolis and Red Peppers   53
    Pepperoni Bread
    Green Salad
    Stuffed Oranges

Venison Chops with Mustard Butter   56
    Roast Potatoes with Rosemary
    Green Beans and Beet Salad
    Coffee Granita

Venison Steak with Wild Mushrooms   60
    Blue Cheese Polenta
    Spinach and Bibb Lettuce Salad
    Strawberry Ice

Venison Steaks Marinated   63
    Grilled Red Pepper Salad
    Mashed Potatoes with Fresh Basil
    Vanilla Ice Cream with Homemade Butterscotch Sauce

Grilled Venison Steak with Rosemary Butter   69
    Bibb Lettuce and Tomato Salad
    White Bean Purée
    Coffee Ice Cream and Hazelnut Liqueur

Venison Chops with Blue Cheese and Caraway Seeds   71
    Sweet Potato Gratin
    Braised Fennel
    Fresh Figs

Venison Steak with Red Wine   74
    Bittergreens and Cheese Salad
    Garlic Toasts
    Rhubarb Tart

Venison Calzone   80
    Sliced Tomatoes with Basil
    Fried Sage Leaves
    Poached Pears

Venison Chops with Basil Cream   84
    Homemade Pasta with Parsley
    Salad with Hazelnut Dressing
    Brandied Apricots and Crème Anglaise

Game Care   *89*

Index   *97*

About *Gray's Venison Cookbook*

The venison menus that you will find collected here are from *The New Gray's Wild Game Cookbook*, Rebecca Gray's 2009 revision of her best selling *Gray's Wild Game Cookbook* first published in 1983. In the 26 years since that initial edition, the world of bookselling has changed considerably. In those days before the internet, readers tended to find what they wanted by going to a bookstore, looking over the shelves, and selecting a book. Publishers knew it when someone purchased one of their books from that shelf, but that's all they knew. They had no way of knowing what sent the reader looking there in the first place. Now, while many still browse bookstore shelves in person, many more do their searching online, and by making those electronic searches, book buyers let publishers know what they're looking for.

A lot of you have been looking for this book: a shorter, handier, venison-only collection of Rebecca's elegant menus.

Here it is. We hope you enjoy it.

The Editors

Venison

I haven't always known about cooking venison. A culinary confrontation with a piece of venison in the late 1960s got me going: a white-tailed deer steak that mysteriously appeared at the Tufts University fraternity house in Boston where a boyfriend lived and where I spent a lot of time. This was back before college-age men thought it was cool to be a good cook and so the task of preparing food unquestioningly fell to the woman on hand—in this case, me. I recall there were deer hairs on the steak, a clear sign that the last person who'd handled the meat knew even less than I did about game prep. But while I carefully picked each hair off, I noticed something else: Despite whatever it had been through, it was absolutely beautiful, rich, lean meat. I don't remember—likely because it was pretty unmemorable—how I actually cooked it or even how the venison tasted. Fraternity evenings have a way of provoking forgetfulness, but still this void in my culinary knowledge, and probably some vague sense that venison could be spectacular eating, piqued my curiosity: How *do* you prepare venison?

The fraternity venison incident also foreshadowed what was to come—initially a necessary learning process, but eventually a life-long passion. In 1975 I married a hunter and fisherman, and the same year of our marriage Ed and I started our publication, *Gray's Sporting Journal*. Suddenly I was faced not only with game in my kitchen but with editing a cooking feature for our hunting and fishing magazine. And quickly I was again faced with the preparation conundrums of venison. Only now it wasn't just cooking problems; I had to help tackle the job of cleaning birds or butchering a whole deer carcass. I was into it now—if only for the imperative moral and ethical rationale that you eat what you kill—and committed to learning everything about game, every subtlety of preparing and cooking it.

The word venison is derived from the Latin verb *venari*, to hunt. And in Robin Hood-type olden days, venison actually referred to all game—meat of an animal killed in the chase. Now we're more explicit, defining the deer species as venison. And although it seems less obvious, we include moose, elk, and caribou in the venison group. These are three of the five species of *Cervidae* (antlered herbivores of the *Artiodactyla* order) which are indigenous to North America. The other two are mule and white-tailed deer, whitetails being the dominant and oldest of the North America deer species.

Deer were indispensable to the early Native Americans. Influencing the spiritual, cultural and economic elements of tribal life, venison was also a substantial portion of their diet. At an archeological site in West Virginia indications are that about ninety percent of the meat being eaten there was venison—and it wasn't only everyday fare. At the 1623 wedding of Plymouth Colony Governor William Bradford, the Wampanoag Indians brought gifts of deer. "We had about twelve pasty venison [meat pies], besides others," wrote one of the guests, Emmanuel Altham, "[and] pieces of roast venison and other such good cheer in such quantity that I could wish you some of our share."

There was such heavy deer harvesting in colonial times that by 1800 the herds had been reduced by thirty-five to fifty percent from pre-Columbian estimates. Between the years of 1776 and 1850 the population of Americans increased from 1.5 million to 23 million, all of them consuming vast quantities of wild game. Plus, venison was inexpensive, which added more pressure on the resource. In 1868 venison was actually cheaper to buy than beef or pork and by the 1890s the harvesting of deer—often by market hunters—was unparalleled by any other time in our history.

By the early 1900s, the entire deer population in the U.S. numbered only 500,000. And deer were not the only game being slaughtered: ducks, geese, turkey, grouse, quail and buffalo all faced near-extinction from over-harvesting. In response a federal regulation, the Lacey Act was passed which prohibited interstate commerce of game taken in violation of state law. The Act basically ended the practice of market hunting, thus saving much of our wildlife. So for most of the 20th Century virtually the only way to eat American venison was if you, or a sharing friend, could successfully hunt deer.

The history of venison in Europe was quite different: Venison was the stuff of kings—no democratic freedoms for the masses when it came to deer hunting or consumption. Hunting was strictly controlled by the ruling class, who limited the number of deer harvested and initiated habitat management to secure herd size. Then in the process of colonizing other parts of the world, the Europeans not only found new species of deer, but enjoyed the freedom to hunt them.

In the mid-1800s the British transplanted red, fallow and sika deer to New Zealand, primarily for recreational hunting, and the deer found ideal habitat. They prospered to the point that their exploding population all but denuded the hills of vegetation, causing extensive erosion, habitat loss, and near extinction of some ground-feeding birds. Within a little over a hundred years the deer grew so pervasive they were not only hunted extensively but poisoned as pests. Then some enterprising hunters decided that instead of letting the plentiful deer carcasses just rot, they would sell them to restaurants. This caught the attention of New Zealand farmers and in the first true domestication of a wild species in over 10,000 years, farmers captured and then propagated deer. By 1987 there were 3,500 deer farms in New Zealand and over 860,000 pounds of the Kiwi venison being served in U.S. restaurants.

There'd been a growing desire and interest here in new cuisines and all things culinary, which got its start when World War II troops returned from Europe. First it had to be French, then Italian, then any ethnic, exotic or gourmet food. It was fueled in the 1960s by the television. show of Cordon Bleu-trained Julia Child, and later in the 1980s redefined by Alice Waters' emphasis on artisanal foods of the *terroir*.

Certainly this progression helped drive the demand in the U.S for Euro-exotic venison. From 1990 to 1994 our venison consumption doubled. Sure, venison's popularity was due in large part to our blossoming appreciation of gourmet foods, but also to the burgeoning emphasis on healthy, more natural foods. Venison is high in protein, contains iron, zinc and many of the B vitamins; and it's raised naturally—devoid of growth hormones, antibiotics and dyes. Plus venison is very lean, with one-eighth the fat content of beef and less cholesterol than a skinless chicken breast.

With an increasing demand for venison here in the U.S., the opportunity door was open for a domestic supply to find its way into the marketplace. During the 20th Century there had been an incredible rebound of wild American deer: from a total population of half a million in 1900 to 25 million in 1997. By 2006 the white-tailed deer alone was estimated to be close to 20 million animals. Despite this, the Lacey Act has remained intact, preventing any commercial use of wild game. But the Lacey Act has no jurisdiction over farm-raised animals.

Are there differences between wild and farm-raised deer? Of course. Farm-raised deer are fenced in and more sedentary than their wild counterparts. Plus the constancy of their diet and the slaughterhouse approach to processing the meat all make for a different flavor—farmed venison is a bit flatter, less, well…flavorful. In general, we've domesticated the taste right out of most of our meat, and farmed venison seems headed in that direction.

I admit bias here. Since those early deer days, I'd seized the challenge, grabbed the gauntlet and spent decades learning how to prepare game. And included in my new venison knowledge were techniques and opinions about processing—proper bleeding, cooling, aging, butchering. It was always wild deer and I was picky about it, downright snooty, shuddering at the very memory of my two firsts—the fraternity hair-flecked steak and the cartop deer (see "Game Care," p. 89). Now I knew what made great venison—its wildness made the complexities, subtle nuances of flavor that were unparalleled. And the way we handled it, I'm proud to say, encouraged that nuanced and fabulous taste.

In this book I have not been quite as liberal with the term venison as in the Robin Hood days, but do use the word venison in its broader sense to mean all that are in the deer family: caribou, moose, elk, antelope, white-tail and mule deer. This is a cook's taxonomy, not a biologist's, so all of the venison recipes in this chapter are applicable to these animals. Some slight adjustments in quantities of accompanying ingredients and cooking times should be made to accommodate for a larger size (moose, elk) cut of venison.

Venison Black Bean Chili
Fennel Seed Bread
Baby Spinach and Arugula Salad with Avocado and Egg
Ginger Angel Crisps

Serves eight

VENISON BLACK BEAN CHILI

- 2 cups black beans, dried or 3 16-oz. cans
- ¼ cup oil, approximately
- 1 stalk celery, chopped small
- 2 medium onions, chopped small
- 8 cloves garlic, chopped very fine
- 4 lbs. boneless venison cut in ½-inch cubes
- 1 tsp. salt
- 3 tbsp. dried oregano
- 1 tsp. cayenne pepper
- ½ tsp. ground coriander
- ⅓ cup medium-hot chili powder
- 2 tbsp. ground cumin
- 3½ cups hot chicken stock (use Knorr chicken cubes)
- 1 28-oz. can Italian plum tomatoes
  Approximately 8 cups cooked, short grain, brown rice (or you can use wild rice if you are feeling lavish)
- 3-4 tbsp. chopped parsley for garnish
- 1 cup sour cream mixed with grated rind of 1 lemon to be passed as garnish (optional)

Rinse the dried beans, remove any stones and cover with water in a large pot and bring to a boil. Remove from the heat, cover and let stand several hours. Then drain , cover with water again and cook for 1-2 hours until they are tender but still have some bite. (Some beans are tougher than others, especially ones from health food stores which should definitely be soaked overnight.) If using canned beans, just rinse well and drain.

Heat half of the oil in a large cooking casserole and cook the celery and the onions over medium heat till soft, about 15 minutes. Add the garlic and cook another few minutes, stirring, then remove all from the pan to a small bowl.

Heat the rest of the oil in the same pan, add the meat and cook stirring occasionally until the meat is grey—you do not sear the meat so use medium heat, it should take no longer than 10-15 minutes.

Then return the onion mixture to the pan and add salt, oregano, cayenne, coriander, chili powder, and cumin. Stir to mix and cook another 5 minutes.

Now add the stock and canned tomatoes (break them with a fork) with their juices; bring to a boil. Stir well and simmer uncovered for 2 hours or until the meat is folk-tender.

Stir in the beans and taste for seasoning. You probably will want more salt and oregano. Heat until nice and hot and serve with rice, parsley and/or lemon sour cream.

If you want to thicken the juices, place a tablespoon or so of cornstarch in a glass and mix with a few tablespoons of water. Then add a few teaspoons of the hot chili liquid; one by one. Mix well, pour it all back into the pot and slowly bring to a boil stirring all the time—-then remove from the heat. It should thicken right up. Just remember if you should reheat the chili, do so slowly, so as not to break the starch.

FENNEL SEED BREAD

- 2 cups lukewarm to warm water
- 1 tbsp. dry yeast
- 1 tbsp. sugar
- 1 tbsp. salt
- 2 tbsp. dried fennel seed, plus enough to sprinkle atop each loaf
- 5 cups or so of all-purpose flour (I recommend King Arthur Flour)
- Butter and oil for greasing pans

In the bowl of a standing mix master, fitted with a bread hook, add the warm water and sprinkle in the yeast, sugar, salt, and 2 tbsp. fennel seed. Let sit for a few minutes until the yeast looks dissolved and foamy. Now pour in 5 cups of flour and mix at the lowest setting, usually marked "stir," until the flour is blended and then increase the speed to the next level, #2. Continue blending at this speed until the dough is well mixed, pulling away from the sides of the bowl, and forming a ball. Turn onto a floured surface and knead the dough for about 8 minutes. It should be slightly tacky to the touch but smooth and very malleable. Place in a bowl that has been oiled, turn the dough over in the oil so the top is oiled, too, and cover the bowl with a cloth. Let rise until it is double in size, about 2 to 3 hours. Punch it down and let it rest while you prepare the pan(s) for it to rise in again.

This recipe makes enough for a baguette and a loaf. I always make a baguette for the week's spaghetti night so I pull a handful of dough off and roll it into a big snake and lay it in one side of a baguette pan that has been buttered. The remaining dough I either place into a buttered loaf pan, pushing it into the rectangle shape, or form a ball with the dough, flouring it heavily, and put into a banneton, also heavily floured. Both the baguette and the loaf/round I cover with a cloth and let rise again for another hour or so.

The breads in the metal baking pans can first be sprinkled with fennel seeds and then go directly into a preheated oven at 420° for 35 to 40 minutes until golden brown. The banneton is trickier. I use a piece of parchment paper, floured, atop the back of a cookie sheet and carefully invert the banneton and let the dough fall out. Often it loses its rise and I let it sit covered for another hour to rise again. Once the round is ready to bake I sprinkle it with fennel seeds and slide it onto a pizza stone that is in a preheated oven at 420° and bake it for 40 minutes or until golden. Once baked, I turn the baguette and loaf out of their pans—or slide the round on the parchment onto the cookie sheet—and onto a rack to cool. Let cool for 30 minutes or so before cutting.

If I don't plan to use the baguette that day I wrap it in foil and put it in the freezer to use another day. (It just needs to be taken from the freezer and put in a preheated oven at 350° for 30 minutes or so.)

BABY SPINACH AND ARUGULA SALAD WITH AVOCADO AND EGG

For the vinaigrette:
- 1 tbsp. lemon juice
- 1 tbsp. balsamic vinegar
- ¼ tsp. salt
- Several grinds of the pepper grinder
- 1 tsp. prepared honey mustard
- ¼ cup good green olive oil

For the salad:
- 1 hard-cooked egg
- 1 bag baby spinach leaves
- 1 bag baby arugula
- 1 ripe avocado

Combine all six ingredients for the vinaigrette in a small jar with a lid that fits securely. Make sure the lid is on tight and shake vigorously several times before using it to dress the salad.

Set the egg in water and cook on high for 17 minutes. Remove from the heat and put the egg under cold running water. While the egg is cooking, wash and spin dry both the spinach and arugula and place in a salad bowl. Peel and slice both the egg and the avocado and add it to the spinach/arugula. Dress with the vinaigrette and toss. Add a few grinds of the pepper grinder.

GINGER ANGEL CRISPS

- 1½ cups flour
- ½ tsp. baking soda
- ¼ cup (½ stick) unsalted butter
- ¼ cup sugar
- ½ cup molasses
- ½ tsp. powdered ginger
- Powdered sugar for dusting (about a ½ cup)

In a bowl combine the flour and baking soda and whisk it a few times to mix and set aside. In a medium-size pan bring to a rolling boil the butter, sugar, molasses, and ginger and let it boil a minute or two. Remove from the heat and stir in the flour mixture a little at a time until it is completely incorporated. Let the dough cool just a bit—it should still be very warm to the touch—and take a large spoonful and form into a ball. Set on a lightly floured surface and cover with plastic wrap. Roll out the dough so it is VERY thin. Remove the wrap and using a little angel—or other small form—cookie cutter, cut out the cookies. Place the angels on a cookie sheet lined with parchment paper and cook in a preheated oven at 350° for 4 to 8 minute or until the edges are browning slightly. Remove from the oven and slide the parchment with the cookies onto a cooling rack. Let sit for 5 minutes and then slide Angel Crisps from the paper onto a plate. In a small plastic bag pour a small amount of powdered sugar and add, in batches of 3, the little angel cookies and shake to cover.

Repeat with remaining dough. (After a while you may have to reheat the dough, it needs to be very warm in order to roll it thin.) This makes a good number of cookies—certainly enough for eight people—but the precise number depends on the size of your angels.

Venison Burgers with Chateaubriand Butter
Fried Bread
Vegetable Salad
Fresh Fruit

Serves four

Venison burger is not only delightful to eat, but often your best alternative for the cuts damaged in the field or naturally tougher. If the outfitter has not butchered the deer for you and you fancy doing it yourself, you may find it difficult getting the meat made into burger. If you are a city-dweller and hunting refers to what shoppers do at Bloomie's or Macy's rather than something that goes on in the woods, chances are you will not find a butcher who will grind the meat for you. Even the la-di-da butchers who have gouged you for years and theoretically owe you a favor are bound by the state sanitary codes and don't like to risk any infringement of the law.

Rural butchers are likelier to be able to handle your request to grind the meat and add the pork fat necessary to create burger. If you are going to try to grind it yourself, I make two suggestions. Try to use meat that is very cold—near freezing—and free of any fat or sinew. A food processor works well, as does the meat grinder attachment to a Kitchen Aid mixer. But I once spent a tearful evening, when I was pregnant with our third child and Ed was off hunting, trying to jam big chunks of deer leg meat through a hand-crank meat grinder. It simply did not work. In general grinding meat at home is tedious and better to do in small batches or left to the butcher or outfitter to do.

VENISON BURGERS WITH CHATEAUBRIAND BUTTER

- 1 cup white wine
- 3 shallots chopped very, very fine
- 1 handful of fresh parsley, chopped
- 1 tsp. chervil
- 1 tsp. tarragon
- 1 cup stock
- 1 cup (2 sticks) unsalted butter
- Salt and pepper
- 2 lbs. venison burger (chopped or ground)

In a small saucepan combine the wine, shallot, parsley, chervil, and tarragon and bring it to a boil. Reduce heat and simmer very, very slowly until the liquid has been reduced by half. Add the stock and continue to reduce until ½ cup liquid is left. Whip the butter till soft and add the cooled wine and stock mixture. Season with salt and pepper and wrap in plastic wrap. Shape into a log and freeze one hour or overnight. Form the burger into patties and cook over a grill. Slice several pats of the butter for each burger and serve on top.

FRIED BREAD

    1 loaf French bread
    1 garlic clove
    ½ cup (1 stick) unsalted butter
    Salt to taste

Slice the French bread into 12 ½-inch pieces and dry them on a cookie sheet in a 300° oven. Do not let them cook. If you wish, rub one side of the dried bread with a garlic clove sliced in half. In a heavy-bottomed saucepan, melt the stick of butter, heating it till it sizzles. Put in the bread and brown both sides. Sprinkle with salt if you like.

VEGETABLE SALAD

1 14-oz. can artichoke hearts
½ lb. fava beans
½ lb. peas
½ lb. new potatoes

Drain, rinse and quarter the artichoke hearts. Shell, peel and blanch the fava beans. Plunge into cold water. Shell and blanch the peas. Plunge into cold water. When both fava beans and peas are cool combine with the artichoke. Cook the little potatoes in enough salted boiling water to just cover them for 20 minutes or until tender. Let cool and then quarter them. Add the potatoes to the other vegetables and then toss with a nice herbed vinaigrette.

Saddle of Venison
Potatoes and Porcini
Braised Fennel
Clafoutis

Serves four

It took me years to find out what was meant by a "saddle of venison." I had heard of a rack or a haunch but never a saddle. A saddle of venison is the equivalent of a standing rib roast in beef. It is the middle section of chops left intact to make the premier of roasts. At the point of butchering the saddle can cause the very worst consternation. Whether 'tis nobler to wade through a series of delicious meals of venison chops or to go for the glut of an incredible roast—if you go for the glut we suggest the following recipe.

SADDLE OF VENISON

¼ cup olive oil
1 tbsp. lemon juice
5-6 lbs. saddle of venison
Enough pork lard to cover the saddle
1 tbsp. crushed juniper berries
1 tsp. salt
1 onion, sliced
5 tbsp. unsalted butter
¼ cup red wine vinegar
1 lemon
Sprinkle of flour
Salt and pepper

Combine the oil and lemon juice and rub over the meat. Let it sit for a couple of hours. Lard with 2-inch strips in even rows with pork fat. Mix the juniper berries and salt together and rub over all the larded meat. Sauté the onion in a tablespoon of the butter and lay on the bottom of a roasting pan with the meat on top. Add the vinegar to the pan and baste the meat with the remaining butter, melted. Roast in a preheated oven at 350° for about an hour. Then sprinkle the lard with flour and baste with butter. Cook until the lard is crispy.

Julienne the lemon rind and blanch for 5 minutes in boiling water. Combine with the juices from the roast pan and serve on top of the sliced meat.

POTATOES AND PORCINI

- 2 oz. dried wild mushrooms (morels or porcini are best)
- ½ cup heavy cream
- 1 small garlic clove, minced
- 3 tbsp. unsalted butter
- 2 lbs. boiling potatoes
- Salt and pepper

Soak in warm water for 15 minutes and then rinse the reconstituted mushrooms quickly in cold water using a strainer so any grit will be removed. Chop coarsely and put in a saucepan with the heavy cream. Simmer very slowly until the cream is reduced to ¼ cup and aromatic with the mushrooms. Sauté the garlic in 1 tablespoon of the butter for a moment and add it to the mushroom/cream mixture. Season with salt and pepper and set aside. Peel the potatoes and slice them into ¼-inch slices. Rinse them twice in cold water letting them sit 10 to 15 minutes each time. Strain and dry potatoes. Butter a low earthenware-type casserole. Put in one layer of potatoes and then one layer of mushroom mixture. Make the last layer potatoes and dot with remaining butter. Season with salt and pepper and bake 30 to 40 minutes in a 425° oven.

BRAISED FENNEL

- 4 heads fennel
- 4 tbsp. unsalted butter, plus enough to butter the pan and parchment
- 1 cup stock
- Salt and pepper
- ½ cup gruyere cheese, grated

Trim, core and cut in half the four fennel heads. Butter a baking dish and arrange the fennel in it. Add 4 tablespoons of butter, stock, salt, and pepper and cover with buttered parchment paper. Cook in a preheated oven at 400° for 30 minutes. Remove the paper and continue cooking for 10 minutes. The stock should have reduced some. Now add the cheese and cook until it is melted and brown.

CLAFOUTIS

- ¾ cup milk
- ½ cup flour
- 1 tsp. vanilla (or grated lemon or orange rind)
- Pinch of salt
- 2 eggs
- ¼ cup granulated sugar
- 1 lb. cherries, pitted (or use any good fruit)
- Confectioners' sugar

Mix the milk, flour, vanilla or rind, salt, eggs and 2 tablespoons of the granulated sugar together. Butter an oven-proof serving dish and pour a third of the batter in it. Bake that for 10 minutes at 375°. Remove from the oven and add the fruit and sprinkle with the remaining sugar. Pour in the rest of the batter and continue cooking in the oven for 30 minutes. Sprinkle with confectioners' sugar and cut into pie-shaped wedges.

Venison Strip Steaks
Fried Potato Skins
Grilled Red Pepper Salad
Strawberry Ice Cream

Serves four

One of the issues with writing a game cookbook is that occasionally both the highly descriptive or rigidly precise instructions simply do not adequately convey how to accomplish the intended results. Such is the case when trying to communicate "doneness" of meat. Cooking time is always an approximate in cookbooks, especially when game is concerned, and should not be taken as the gospel. Try pressing the meat to see if it has a springy touch to it; then it's done. Wiggle a leg to see if it's loose; then it's done. Or cut into it if you're uncertain (better a slice in it than to serve it too rare or over-cooked). Enviable is a knowledgeable chef's ability to smell doneness. Experience and calling on all of your five senses to determine doneness are a more reliable guide in deciding if dinner is ready than what is printed in these pages, as much as I hate to admit it. I have put cooking times in only as a general guide on how long to gauge the cocktail hour. But always check for doneness as the cooking process progresses.

VENISON STRIP STEAKS

- 4 thin strip steaks (about ⅓ to ½ lb. each)
- 2 tbsp. oil
- ¼ cup cognac
- ½ cup veal stock
- 4 tbsp. unsalted butter
- 16 capers, large ones, loosely packed in brine
- Salt and pepper

Pan fry the steaks in oil a minute or two on each side or until done and remove to a plate. Deglaze the pan with cognac and add the stock. Reduce the liquid to ¼ cup liquid and whisk in the butter. Rinse the capers well and add to the sauce. Slice the steak, pour the juices into the sauce and season with salt and pepper. Pour the sauce over the meat.

FRIED POTATO SKINS

  5 potatoes
3-5 tbsp. unsalted butter
  ½ garlic clove, chopped (optional)
  1 tsp. parsley, chopped fine
      Salt

Peel the skin off the potatoes using a potato peeler or a knife if you wish to retain more of the potato. Fry in the hot butter and garlic until crisp. Add more butter if needed. Sprinkle with the chopped parsley and sprinkle with salt.

GRILLED RED PEPPER SALAD

  2-3 red peppers
    2 cloves garlic, peeled
    1 cup good green olive oil
       Baby spinach leaves or lettuce, washed
       Vinaigrette

Halve the red peppers and take out the seeds. Place them cut-side down on a piece of foil in the broiler and broil them 2 to 3 minutes till they are black. Remove and let cool. Peel the black skin off, remove any seeds and slice the peppers into pieces. Put in a jar with the garlic cloves and olive oil and let stand at least overnight. Toss with lettuce and your favorite vinaigrette. They are good in sandwiches and will last a week.

STRAWBERRY ICE CREAM

- 4 egg yolks
- ½ cup sugar
- Pinch of salt
- 1½ cups medium cream
- 2 tsp. framboise or vanilla extract
- 6 cups berries (your ice cream will only taste as good as the berries used)
- (Enough ice and salt for the ice cream machine)

Beat together the egg yolks, sugar, and salt till they are smooth but do not ribbon. Add 1 cup cream and mix well. Put over a medium heat stirring constantly until the custard thickens. Remove from the heat, strain and whisk till cool. Add framboise or vanilla and chill. Purée the strawberries. Blend with the custard and add the remaining ½ cup of cream. Churn in ice cream machine according to the manufacturer's directions. Serve with fresh strawberries on top.

Venison Stew
Homemade Pasta
Crusted Blueberry and Cream Cake

Serves four

One of the common bonds between those who cook and those who hunt is that both avocations lead to the accumulation of equipment. It is so nice to have exactly the right little tool to accomplish the task either in the field or in the kitchen. It also could send you to the poorhouse. It is very nice indeed to own an electric pasta machine, but it is not necessary to making very good homemade pasta. It is very nice to own a choice of three deer rifles, but you can only hunt with one at a time. Use what you already own and upgrade when you know your passions.

VENISON STEW

- 2 cups red wine
- ½ cup vinegar
- 1 onion, sliced
- 1 carrot, sliced
- A few parsley stems
- 8 juniper berries
- 1 tbsp. salt
- 1 bay leaf
- 2 crushed cloves
- 4 sprigs tarragon
- 3-4 lbs. venison stew meat
- 4 tbsp. unsalted butter
- ¼ lb. pancetta, diced
- 1½ cup stock (about)
- 1 tbsp. cornstarch
- Salt and pepper

Make a marinade out of the wine, vinegar, onion, carrot, parsley stems, juniper berries, salt, bay leaf, cloves and tarragon sprigs and let the cubed venison sit in it at least overnight.

Drain the marinade from the meat and reserve it. Dry and brown the meat in butter and diced pancetta then cover by ⅔ with the marinade and stock. Cover first with foil pressed close to the meat and bringing it over the sides of the pot. And then add a lid and simmer for about an hour. Test for doneness with a skewer. Remove the meat to a bowl and strain the liquid, discarding the bay leaf, and thicken with cornstarch. Season with salt and pepper and the liquid to the pan and reheat with the meat. Serve.

HOMEMADE PASTA

1½ cups semolina
2 eggs
All-purpose flour for dusting
Salt
Couple of drops of olive oil for the boiling water
2 tbsp. unsalted butter, melted

Make a mountain of the semolina on the counter-top and then make a crater in the mountain. Lightly beat the eggs together and pour into the crater. With a fork bring the semolina into the egg mixture slowly until all the semolina is moist, then form into two small balls. If the dough is at all sticky, add more semolina—the dough needs to be very dry. Knead for 10-20 minutes and then shape into two 8-inch-long (or so) snakes. Cut each snake into 6 pieces. Take one of the pieces and knead it for a few minutes. Flatten with the palm of your hand until it is thin enough to crank through the pasta machine on the thickest setting (#1 on the classic machine). Fold the pasta and crank through again. Repeat this two more times on this setting. Now put the pasta sheet through each progressive setting on the machine without folding it until the pasta sheet is the desired thickness. For me, this is usually after the second to the last setting (#5). Finally cut the pasta and lay on a floured cutting board and sprinkle with all-purpose flour. Toss pasta with your fingers so it is well dusted with the flour. Repeat the procedure for the remaining pieces of dough. The pasta may now be left to dry.

Of course dried pasta can be stored or cooked immediately. Fresh pasta cooks very quickly in boiling water—be sure to add salt to the water and a drop of oil—only about 2 to 3 minutes. Drain and toss with melted butter or reduced cream.

CRUSTED BLUEBERRY AND CREAM CAKE

For the cake:

- 1 quart blueberries
- 1⅓ cups all-purpose flour
- 1 tsp. dry yeast
- Pinch of salt
- 4 eggs
- ¾ cup sugar
- 1 tsp. vanilla

For the syrup:

- 1⅓ cups sugar
- ¼ cup water
- 2 tbsp. Grand Marnier
- ⅓ cup boiling water
- Whipped cream

Butter a 10-inch spring-form pan and cut a round of parchment paper to fit the bottom. Butter the paper, too, and dust both with flour.

Rinse the blueberries. Set aside.

Sift together the flour, yeast, and salt. (If need be, pulverize the yeast in a mortar before sifting.)

Over a very gentle heat, whisk eggs and sugar until quite warm, but don't allow the eggs to set around the edges. Place the eggs/sugar mixture and vanilla in a large metal mixer bowl. Continue beating by machine until the mixture mounts to a thick, almost white foam that forms a ribbon and has at least tripled in volume. Place a dense but single layer of blueberries into the spring-form pan. Pour on half the batter, sprinkle on remaining berries and cover with the rest of the batter. Bake in a preheated oven at 350° for 40 minutes.

Prepare a caramel syrup. Place 1 cup sugar and ¼ cup water in a small heavy pan over medium heat. Stir just until the sugar is dissolved, then leave alone. Let the sugar gently bubble until it starts to turn first to straw, then to deeper shades of yellow and gold and then finally to amber. Remove from heat and cool slightly. Add liqueur and ⅓ cup boiling water to make a pourable syrup.

Test cake for "doneness" by inserting a knife in the center. It should come out clean. Unmold on a serving platter and pour warm caramel syrup over the blueberried top. Sprinkle a layer of granulated sugar (about ⅓ cup) evenly over the cake and place briefly under a broiler until the sugar crystallizes into a crisp topping. Serve with whipping cream.

Venison Stew with Artichoke Hearts and Sun-dried Tomatoes
Basil Bread
Green Salad
Custard Oranges

Serves four

One year we were made a present of 50 pounds of venison, already butchered, wrapped and frozen. We didn't know the hunters or the outfitter or the butcher or even from what part of the world the deer came from. It was the first time I realized how valuable it is to be able to listen to the long, drawn-out tales of how the buck got bagged and dragged before you have to go in the kitchen and cook it. Previously, I'd always had the privilege of staring glassy-eyed at the hunter while my subconscious soaked up the pertinent details of how big and old the deer was, how clean was the shot, and what type of terrain the deer lived in. And I had been rather mechanical in applying that knowledge to my choice of recipes for the meat (see Chapter on "Game Care," 89). I learned my lesson; I certainly had a hard time figuring out what to do with those 50 pounds of meat to make them taste decent. If you can't be there yourself, at least ask a lot of questions.

The following is a recipe I would use on good quality stew meat, either a neck roast from a large deer or the shank roast from a smaller deer, cut up.

VENISON STEW WITH ARTICHOKE HEARTS AND SUN-DRIED TOMATOES

1½ lbs. venison stew meat
4 tbsp. oil
1 small onion
1 small carrot
3 cups good red wine
1 cup stock
Bouquet garni
½ cup sun-dried tomatoes
2 14 oz. cans (or two boxes frozen) artichoke hearts
1 tbsp. cornstarch
6 tbsp. butter
Salt and pepper
1 tbsp. chopped parsley
1 tbsp. grated lemon rind
1 small garlic clove, chopped fine

Brown the meat in the oil and remove from the pan. Chop the onion and carrot and sauté in the pan where the meat was. Return the meat and add the wine and stock to the pot. Bring to a boil and add the bouquet garni and sun-dried tomatoes. Soak the canned artichoke hearts for a while in cold water to remove the brine taste (this is unnecessary if they are frozen) and then add them to the pot. Cover the pan with foil, pressing down so there is no space between the foil and liquid. Put the lid on and simmer for about 20 minutes or until a skewer comes out easily and cleanly from a piece of the meat. When done, drain the juices into a frying pan and thicken with cornstarch. Whisk in the butter and season with salt and pepper. Return the meat and add the parsley, garlic and lemon rind. Check for seasoning and serve.

BASIL BREAD

- 2 cups lukewarm to warm water
- 1 tbsp. dry yeast
- 1 tbsp. sugar
- 1 tbsp. salt
- 2 tbsp. dried basil
- 5 cups or so of all-purpose flour (I recommend King Arthur Flour)
- Butter and oil for greasing pans

In the bowl of a standing mix master, fitted with a bread hook, add the warm water and sprinkle in the yeast, sugar, salt, and basil. Let sit for a few minutes until the yeast looks dissolved and foamy. Now pour in 5 cups of flour and mix at the lowest setting, usually marked "stir," until the flour is blended and then increase the speed to the next level, #2. Continue blending at this speed until the dough is well mixed, pulling away from the sides of the bowl, and forming a ball. Turn onto a floured surface and knead the dough for about 8 minutes. It should be slightly tacky to the touch but smooth and very malleable. Place in a bowl that has been oiled, turn the dough over in the oil so the top is oiled, too, and cover the bowl with a cloth. Let rise until it is double in size, about 2 to 3 hours. Punch it down and let it rest while you prepare the pan(s) for it to rise in again.

This recipe makes enough for a baguette and a loaf. I always make a baguette for the week's spaghetti night so I pull a handful of dough off and roll it into a big snake and lay it in one side of a baguette pan that has been buttered. The remaining dough I either place into a buttered loaf pan, pushing it into the rectangle shape, or form a ball with the dough, flouring it heavily, and put into a banneton, also heavily floured. Both the baguette and the loaf/round I cover with a cloth and let rise again for another hour or so.

The breads in the metal baking pans can go directly into a preheated oven at 420° for 35 to 40 minutes until golden brown. The banneton is trickier. I use a piece of parchment paper, floured, atop the back of a cookie sheet and careful invert the banneton and let the dough fall out. Often it loses its rise and I let it sit covered for another hour to rise again. Once the round is ready to bake I slide it onto a pizza stone that is in a preheated oven at 420° and bake it for 40 minutes or until golden. Once baked, I turn the baguette and loaf out of their pans—or slide the round on the parchment onto the cookie sheet—and onto a rack to cool. Let cool for 30 minutes or so before cutting.

If I don't plan to use the baguette that day I wrap it in foil and put it in the freezer to use another day. (It just needs to be taken from the freezer and put in a preheated oven at 350° for 30 minutes or so.)

CUSTARD ORANGES

    4 large navel oranges
    3 egg yolks
    ⅓ cup sugar
  1½ oz. Cointreau
  1⅓ cup heavy cream

Cut off the top of each orange and scoop out the inside. Rinse and let drain. Beat the egg yolks and sugar together then add the Cointreau. Now whip 1 cup of the cream until it is stiff. Stir in ⅓ of the whipped cream and then fold in the rest of the whipped cream. Fill each orange with the egg-cream mixture and set on a plate in the refrigerator for at least two hours. When ready to serve whip the remaining ⅓ cup cream and put a dollop on each orange top. Dust with cocoa.

Venison with Port
Roast Potatoes
Sautéed Watercress
Meyer Lemon Sherbet

Serves four

VENISON WITH PORT

   Pork lard (enough to cover the saddle in 2-inch strips)
4-5 lbs. saddle of venison (see page 26)
 4 carrots
 4 onions
  A few parsley stems
 ⅔ cup unsalted butter
 2 cups port
 ½ tsp. powdered cloves
 ½ tsp. cinnamon

Preheat the oven to 500°. Lard the saddle and tie with string to hold in place. Peel and chop fine the carrots, onions and parsley stems. Sauté them all in 6 tablespoons of the butter. Lay the vegetables on the bottom of a roasting pan and put the venison on top. Pour the port over it and cook for about 10 minutes. Lower the heat to 400° and continue to cook for another half hour or so basting every 10 minutes. Remove the meat from the pan, skim off any fat and, on top of the stove, reduce the liquid that's left to about half a cup. Add the clove and cinnamon and whisk in the remaining butter and juices which might have exuded from the sliced meat. Check for salt and pepper and serve over slices of the meat.

SAUTÉED WATERCRESS

    3 bunches of watercress, washed and spun dry
    3-4 tbsp. unsalted butter
    Salt and pepper

Take each bunch of watercress and cut into 2-inch lengths (the bunches should be cut approximately into thirds). Sauté the watercress in the hot unsalted butter for a second or two then put on the lid for two minutes. Remove the lid, season with salt and pepper and a little more butter, and serve.

MEYER LEMON SHERBET

- 7-8 Meyer lemons (to make 1 cup of juice)
- 1½ cups sugar
- 1½ cups water
- 1 tbsp. at least Meyer lemon rind, slivered and chopped fine
- ¾ cup whole milk
- 2 tbsp. water
- 1 tsp. gelatin
- (Enough kosher salt and ice cubes for your ice cream machine)

Juice the Meyer lemons, making sure you have a full cup, and reserve the rind from one of the lemons. In a small saucepan combine the sugar and water and heat until the sugar is completely dissolved. Sliver the lemon rind and chop fine. In a bowl, pour the sugar water and the lemon juice and add in the milk and lemon rind. In the saucepan put the 2 tablespoons of water and stir in the gelatin and let it sit until the gelatin has plumped up-about a minute or two. Then heat it gently so there is no graininess. Stir in the gelatin now to the lemon-milk mixture, cover the bowl with plastic wrap, and refrigerate for at least six hours until it is very cold. Then freeze it according to the instructions with your ice cream maker.

Venison Scallops
Persillade Potatoes
Green Beans
Tarte Tatin

Serves four

VENISON SCALLOPS

- 2 tbsp. coarsely chopped hazelnuts
- 3 tbsp. oil
- Rind from one quarter of an orange
- 8-10 venison scallops (slice ½-inch pieces of meat from a good cut of roast, like the eye of the round, making sure to cut across the grain).
- ¼ cup Armagnac
- 1 cup stock
- ¼ cup plus 1 tbsp. unsalted butter
- Salt and pepper

Toast the nuts in the oven till they are light brown. Wrap in a towel for 10 minutes to create steam and to loosen the skin from the nut, rub off the skins and sauté in 1 tablespoon oil. Chop fine.

Remove the orange rind (making sure to get no pith) from the orange with a potato peeler and julienne into slivers. Blanch for 5 minutes in boiling water. Rinse, drain and reserve.

Pan fry the scalloped venison in 2 tablespoons of oil for a minute or two on each side. Remove from the pan and set aside. Deglaze the pan with Armagnac and then add the stock and reduce the liquid to ¼ cup. Whisk in the butter and season with salt and pepper. Add the nuts and orange slivers and serve over the venison scallops.

PERSILLADE POTATOES

  2 garlic cloves
½ bunch parsley
  2 large potatoes
  2 tbsp. bacon fat or butter
     Salt and pepper

Chop the garlic and parsley fine and mix together. Peel and slice the potatoes very thin and then sauté them in bacon fat over a medium heat with the lid on for five minutes. Remove the lid and add the parsley and garlic mixture and cook for a few more minutes. Season with salt and pepper and serve.

TARTE TATIN

- 6 hard cooking apples (uncommon apples like Calville Blanc d'Hiver or Esopus Spitzenberg are my favorite for this recipe, but Baldwins or Cortlands work too)
- ¾ cup sugar, plus a sprinkle
- ½ cup water
- 2 tbsp. unsalted butter
- Sprinkle of cinnamon
- 1 sheet Pepperidge Farm Puff Pastry, or your own pastry
- Lightly whipped cream

Peel and slice the apples thinly. Next caramelize the sugar by cooking the water and ¾ cup sugar in a frying pan until it is light brown. Remove immediately from the heat as it will continue to cook and transfer to a cake tin. Spread the caramelized sugar over the bottom and lay the apple slices in concentric circles on top. Only the first layer will show so be sure to make that your best. Dot each layer with butter and sprinkle with sugar and cinnamon. Once the pan is full roll out the pastry and cover the apples with it. Cut a few tiny holes in the pastry to let the steam escape. Cook in the middle of a preheated oven at 450° for 20 minutes. Then turn the heat down to 350° and continue to cook for 30 to 40 minutes. Remove and let cool for a few minutes and then invert onto a serving plate. If it has hardened too much, put the cake tin on a burner and re-melt the caramel. Then invert.

You can add a bit of the extra juices that may run out, once cooled, to the lightly whipped cream.

Venison Chops with Pignolis and Red Peppers
Pepperoni Bread
Green Salad
Stuffed Oranges

Serves four

When I was a child, unsalted butter made me lose my appetite; it simply did not seem right. As an adult I never use salted butter. Of course, historically salt was added to butter to mask any rancidity. And from what I can tell that is still the only reason for adding it to butter, save some lurking childhood biases. Unsalted butter can be more expensive but can be easily justified by treating it as a healthier alternative. Who needs more salt in their diet?

VENISON CHOPS WITH PIGNOLIS AND RED PEPPERS

- 1 sweet red pepper
- 2 tbsp. unsalted butter
- ¼ cup pignolis (pine nuts)
- ¼ cup walnut oil
- 4 venison chops
- Salt and pepper

Cut the red pepper and take the seeds out. Slice into thin strips and sauté in the butter. Sauté the pignolis nuts separately in 2 tablespoons of the walnut oil. Toss the peppers and nuts together and set aside.

Sauté the chops in the remaining walnut oil for a minute or two on each side. Place on plates and add the pepper and nut mixture to the top of each chop. Season with salt and pepper to taste.

PEPPERONI BREAD

- 2 cups lukewarm to warm water
- 1 tbsp. dry yeast
- 1 tbsp. sugar
- 1 tbsp. salt
- 5 cups all-purpose flour
- ⅔ cup pepperoni, chopped
- Butter or oil for greasing pans

In the bowl of a standing mix master, fitted with a bread hook, add the warm water and sprinkle in the yeast, sugar, and salt. Let sit for a few minutes until the yeast looks dissolved and foamy. Now pour in 5 cups of flour and mix at the lowest setting, usually marked "stir," until the flour is blended and then increase the speed to the next level, #2. Continue blending at this speed until the dough is well mixed, pulling away from the sides of the bowl, and forming a ball. Add the chopped pepperoni to the dough. Turn onto a floured surface and knead the dough for about 8 minutes. It should be slightly tacky to the touch but smooth and very malleable. Place in a bowl that has been oiled, turn the dough over in the oil so the top is oiled, too, and cover the bowl with a cloth. Let rise until it is double in size, about 2 to 3 hours. Punch it down and let it rest while you prepare the pan(s) for it to rise in again.

This recipe makes enough for a baguette and a loaf. I always make a baguette for the week's spaghetti night so I pull a handful of dough off and roll it into a big snake and lay it in one side of a baguette pan that has been buttered. The remaining dough I used to make the Pepperoni bread for this menu by forming a ball with the dough, flouring it heavily, and putting it into a banneton, also heavily floured. Both the baguette and the round I cover with a cloth and let rise again for another hour or so.

Using a banneton can be a bit tricky but it produces a beautiful round of bread. Using a piece of parchment paper, floured, atop the back of a cookie sheet, I carefully invert the banneton and let the dough fall out. Often it loses its rise and I let it sit covered for another hour to rise again. Once the round is ready to bake I slide it onto a pizza stone that is in a preheated oven at 420° and bake it and the baguette for 35 to 40 minutes or until golden. Once baked, I turn the baguette out onto a cooling rack and slide the round on the parchment onto the cookie sheet—and also onto the rack to cool. Let cool for 30 minutes or so before cutting.

If I don't plan to use the baguette that day I wrap it in foil and put it in the freezer to use another day. (It just needs to be taken from the freezer and put in a preheated oven at 350° for 30 minutes or so.) .

STUFFED ORANGES

4 large navel oranges
1 qt. orange ice or sherbet
Sprigs of mint

Cut off the top of each orange and scoop out the orange and pith inside. Rinse and let drain. Soften the sherbet or ice and then fill each orange shell. Refreeze and then decorate with sprigs of mint.

Venison Chops with Mustard Butter
Roast Potatoes with Rosemary
Green Beans and Beet Salad
Coffee Granita

Serves four

In many of the recipes I have listed veal stock as an ingredient. Veal stock is not something that can be easily bought—even my old standby game purveyor, D'Artagnan, who always has everything, lists only a duck and veal demi-glace and is out of stock a lot. Although expensive and time-consuming, it is not difficult to make and is very, very worth doing. For many great cooks, it's a once-a-month ritual, and the 12-hour simmer can even take place while you sleep. After it has become a part of your life it will be like hunting: The extra time and effort is simply not remembered, only how good it is. (See page 66.)

VENISON CHOPS WITH MUSTARD BUTTER

- 4 venison chops
- 1 tbsp. oil
- ¼ cup cognac
- ¼ cup veal stock
- ½ cup heavy cream
- 1 tbsp. prepared course-grained mustard
- Salt and pepper

Pan fry the chops in oil and set aside. Deglaze the pan with cognac and add the veal stock and cream. Reduce to half the quantity, remove from heat, and whisk in any juices that have oozed from the resting chops. Add the mustard. Season to taste with salt and pepper and serve over the chops.

ROAST POTATOES WITH ROSEMARY

16 little red potatoes
4 tbsp. melted, unsalted butter
Rosemary
Salt and pepper

Paint the potatoes with the melted butter and sprinkle liberally with rosemary. Roast in the oven for about 45 minutes at 350° or until they are tender. Season with salt and pepper.

GREEN BEANS AND BEET SALAD

- 1 lb. green beans
- 8 medium-size beets
- 1 tbsp. vinegar
- 1 tsp. prepared mustard
- ½ cup olive or walnut oil
- Splash of soy sauce
- Salt and pepper
- Lettuce
- Mint

Blanch the beans in salted boiling water until they are just tender. Plunge them into ice water to stop the cooking and preserve the color. Drain them and let dry. Steam the beets until they are tender and can be pierced with a fork (about half an hour). Let them cool, peel and julienne them. Make a vinaigrette by combining in a blender the vinegar, mustard, oil, soy sauce, salt and pepper. Pour half the vinaigrette on the beets and half on the beans and toss each separately, as the beets will bleed if you toss them too much together. Then toss the two vegetables together gently and serve on a bed of lettuce with a sprig of mint on each serving.

COFFEE GRANITA

1½ cups strong espresso coffee (Italian roasted)
2 tbsp. sugar
Heavy cream

If the coffee is not strong enough let it infuse with the grounds for ½ hour or so. Then strain. Dissolve the sugar in the coffee and chill. Then freeze in ice trays or a brownie tin, stirring every 15 minutes or so for about 3 hours. Serve immediately with cream or whipped cream. Coffee Granita is not meant to be a solid ice. It should be melt-in-your-mouth texture.

Venison Steak with Wild Mushrooms
Blue Cheese Polenta
Spinach and Bibb Lettuce Salad
Strawberry Ice

Serves four

For many years I worked on the food photography for *Gray's Sporting Journal* and then later on the food photography for several of my books. The process always focused on how to achieve the most attractive food presentation. What the eye perceives as being luscious becomes so to the taste buds, too. It is an art, and although published food photos are labored over by professional photographers and stylists, I have seen equal creativity in the practiced cook. Venison, of course, can present its own unique problems for pleasant presentation at the table. But the extra moments spent taking a pair of tweezers to the meat to remove the last hair is worth more to the assurance of a tasty meal than any exotic recipe.

VENISON STEAK WITH WILD MUSHROOMS

 1 oz. dried wild mushrooms
 1 cup cream
 2 lbs. venison steak
 1 tbsp. oil
 ¼ cup cognac or Armagnac
 ⅓ cup veal stock
 Salt and pepper

Soak the mushrooms in warm water for about 15 minutes and then rinse and put into a sauté pan with the cream. Bring it to a boil and then turn it down to a slow simmer. Continue to simmer until the cream is reduced by half.

Pan fry the steak in the oil and remove to a plate to let rest. Deglaze the pan with cognac and add the veal stock. Bring to a boil and let reduce by half. Add the cream and mushroom mixture and any juices that have exuded from the resting steak and let simmer together for a few minutes. Season with salt and pepper and serve over the sliced meat.

BLUE CHEESE POLENTA

- 1 small onion (optional)
- 6 tbsp. unsalted butter
- 2 cups milk
- ¾ cup cornmeal
- 5 oz. blue cheese, diced
- ½ tsp. nutmeg
- 2 tsp. kosher salt
- ½ cup heavy cream
- Pepper

If you are using the onion, sauté it in 2 tablespoons of the butter until translucent. Then, in a small saucepan bring the onion, remaining butter, and milk to a boil. Add the cornmeal slowly, stirring constantly till thick and the spoon can stand up in it. Be careful as the polenta will spit at you. Now add the cheese, nutmeg and salt. Remove from the heat and beat in the cream and pepper. Turn immediately into buttered muffin tins and let rest till set. Remove from the tin and put in a heavy oven-proof pan and cook at 400° for 15 minutes. (If you like, you can add a little more cheese to the tops of the polenta muffins before putting them in the oven.)

STRAWBERRY ICE

6 cups strawberries (approximately)
1 cup sugar
   Pinch of salt and a squirt of lemon juice if needed
1 tbsp. Kirsch
   (Remember to have enough ice and salt for your ice cream freezer, too.)

Wash and hull the strawberries. Purée in the blender. You should have about 1 quart of purée. Boil half a cup of water and add the sugar and cook for 5 minutes. Let cool. Add the sugar syrup to the fruit juice as needed to please your taste. Add salt and lemon juice to help the taste if need be and then pour in the Kirsch. Chill the mixture in the canister from your ice cream maker. Then freeze according to the ice cream machine's directions.

Venison Steaks Marinated
Grilled Red Pepper Salad
Mashed Potatoes with Fresh Basil
Vanilla Ice Cream with Homemade Butterscotch Sauce

Serves four

Twenty-five years ago when I wrote my first cookbook I was careful, where applicable, to always include: "remove the bay leaf" in the instructions. Of course, every cookbook instructs bay leaf removal before serving and I wondered why? Back then when I questioned my cooking teacher, she said that bay leaves are not digested and their sharp edges can actually perforate the stomach wall. Now older and less intimidated by a cooking professional, I decided this sounded perhaps a bit over the top and did a little Wikipedia research. I found nothing about perforated stomachs but rather "the oft-repeated belief that bay leaves should be removed from food after cooking because they are poisonous. This is not true—bay leaves are safe to eat. However, they remain very stiff even after thorough cooking, and because of this, they are not considered culinarily acceptable, and could even pose a potential choking hazard." Whether it's a problem with a perforated stomach or potential for choking, better take that bay leaf out!

VENISON STEAKS MARINATED

- 25-30 juniper berries, lightly toasted and crushed
- Lemon zest from 2 lemons
- 1 tsp. celery salt
- 10 peppercorns, crushed
- 2 tbsp. ground coriander seed
- 1 bay leaf, crumbled
- 2½ cups olive oil
- Juice from 2 lemons (about ⅓ cup)
- 2 lbs. venison steak
- 2 tbsp. unsalted butter
- ¼ cup cognac
- ⅔ cup veal stock
- ½ cup heavy cream
- 2 tsp. sour cream
- Salt and pepper

In a blender, or with a mortar and pestle, blend the juniper berries, lemon rind, celery salt, peppercorns, and coriander seed. Add this to the oil, bay leaf, and lemon juice and marinate the steak overnight.

Wipe the steak dry and pan fry it in butter. Remove the meat and let rest. Deglaze the pan with cognac and then add the veal stock. Bring to a boil and reduce ¼ of the liquid. Add the heavy cream and continue to let it boil and reduce. Add any juices that have exuded from the steak while it has been resting and after it has been carved. Remove the sauce from the heat and whisk in salt and pepper and the sour cream. Serve over the steak.

MASHED POTATOES WITH FRESH BASIL

    4 medium-size potatoes (russet)
½ cup (1 stick) unsalted butter, softened and cut into pats
½ cup or so of the reserved cooking water
      Fresh basil to taste
      Salt and pepper to taste

Wash, peel, and quarter the potatoes. Put the potatoes in cold salted water and bring them to a boil and cook till they are soft when you insert a fork, about 20 minutes. Remove them from the water, reserving half a cup, and push the potatoes through a sieve or potato ricer into a bowl. Add the butter and reserved water and whisk till fluffy. Chop the basil and add it with the salt and pepper to the potatoes and taste.

If you are trying to hold the potatoes, put them in a double boiler, uncovered, and save half of the butter and water to add at the last minute.

VEAL STOCK

- 6 lbs. veal shank
- 3 lbs. veal trimmings
- 3 lbs. veal bones
- 4 large onions, not peeled, with a clove stuck in one
- 3-4 carrots, peeled
- 3 cups white wine
- 2 tsp. salt
- Peppercorns
- Parsley Stems
- Bay leaf
- Thyme

In the oven and in several batches, brown the meat. It is best to do in a large roasting pan. Don't let the bottom burn. Add a little water if necessary as you go along.

Put all meat in a large stock pot. Add the bones, onions, and carrots.

In the roasting pan where the meat was browned add water and wine to cover the dried meat juices to a level of about 1 inch. Bring this to a boil on top of the stove scraping the sides and bottom with a whisk. When the juice is just a ½-inch layer on the bottom of the pan add it to the stock pot with the meat and vegetables.

Fill the rest of the pot with water to cover the meat and vegetables.

Bring to a boil and then turn down to a simmer. Add 2 teaspoons of salt, several peppercorns, parsley stems, bay leaf, and thyme.

Cook 12 hours adding boiling water as necessary to keep the stock level up. Strain through a colander lined with a wet piece of cheesecloth. Skim off the fat and cook down to ⅓ in quantity and let cool again to room temperature. Freeze in ice cube trays. Once frozen remove with a knife and store cubes in plastic bags.

Do not let the stock sit long at room temperature or it will sour. And never let it sit at room temperature with the bones in; always strain them out even if you have to stop the cooking in the middle, only to restart later. Meat stock is fertile ground for bacteria.

GRILLED RED PEPPER SALAD

- 2-3 red peppers
- 2 cloves garlic, peeled
- 1 cup good green olive oil

Halve the red peppers and take out the seeds (or use whole). Place them cut-side down on a piece of foil in the broiler and broil them 2 to 3 minutes till they are black. Remove and let cool. Peel the black skin off, remove the seeds and slice the peppers into pieces. Put in a jar with the garlic cloves and olive oil and let stand at least over night. Toss with lettuce and your favorite vinaigrette. These are good in sandwiches, too.

HOMEMADE BUTTERSCOTCH

  2 cups sugar
  ¾ cups water
      Pinch of salt
  2½ cups hot cream
  4 tbsp. unsalted butter (optional)

Make a sugar syrup with the sugar, water, and salt. Cook till light brown. Remove from heat and add the heated cream stirring all the time. For a richer sauce, add the softened butter after the cream.

Grilled Venison Steak with Rosemary Butter
Bibb Lettuce and Tomato Salad
White Bean Purée
Coffee Ice Cream with Hazelnut Liqueur

Serves four

In beef the cut of meat identifies for us the quality of the meat. Unfortunately what we have learned is a great cut of beef is not necessarily paralleled in venison. Venison steaks, for example, are quite often the less desirable cut of meat; the chops the best. Nonetheless, you can't go wrong with a grilled steak.

GRILLED VENISON STEAK WITH ROSEMARY BUTTER

- 2 tsp. dried rosemary
- ½ tsp. garlic, chopped
- ½ cup (1 stick) unsalted butter
- Salt and pepper
- 2 lbs. venison steak

Chop the rosemary and the garlic very fine. Whip the butter and add the rosemary, garlic and salt and pepper to taste. Wrap the butter in plastic wrap and shape into a log. Place in the freezer while you start the charcoal or heat up the gas grill. Once the grill is very hot, cook the steak quickly. Cut slices of the butter to go on top of each serving.

WHITE BEAN PURÉE

- 1 lb. white beans, soaked an hour
- 2½ cups chicken stock
- 2½ cups water
- 1 onion
- 2 cloves
- 1 bay leaf
- Pinch of thyme
- A few parsley stems
- Salt and pepper
- ¾ cup heavy cream
- ½ cup (1 stick) unsalted butter, softened

Drain the soaking beans and pour in the water and broth (if you don't have any chicken stock, all water with chicken bouillon cubes is fine). Peel the onion and push the cloves into it. Add the onion, bay leaf, thyme, parsley stems and salt and pepper to the bean pot and bring to a boil. Simmer until the beans are tender (about a half hour to an hour). Remove bay leaf. In small batches, churn up the bean mixture in a food processor. Zipping it for just a second not to purée, but just to break the skins of the beans. Push through a strainer back into the pot and mix in the cream and butter. Reheat gently and season with salt and pepper.

Venison Chops with Blue Cheese and Caraway Seeds
Sweet Potato Gratin
Braised Fennel
Fresh Figs

Serves four

VENISON CHOPS WITH BLUE CHEESE AND CARAWAY SEEDS

- ½ cup (1 stick) unsalted butter, softened
- 1 tbsp. blue cheese, crumbled
- ½ tsp. crushed caraway seeds
- Few drops of Worcestershire sauce
- Pepper to taste
- 4 chops
- 2½ tbsp. oil

Whip the butter till it is fluffy. Add the cheese, caraway, Worcestershire and pepper and mix well. Roll up in plastic wrap and shape into a log and freeze for at least 1 hour or preferably overnight. Pan fry the chops in oil, about two or three minutes a side (depending on thickness) and place on plates. Slice off two or three pats of the cheese/butter per chop and put them on top to melt over the chops.

SWEET POTATO GRATIN

- 3 white potatoes
- 3 yellow sweet potatoes (or yams)
- 2½ cups cream
- ½ tsp. cognac
- ¼ tsp. nutmeg
- ¼ tsp. powdered cloves
- A pinch of thyme
- Salt and pepper
- (Butter for greasing the dish)

Peel and cut the potatoes into thin ⅛-inch slices. Layer in a buttered baking dish and add the cream, cognac, nutmeg, clove, thyme, and salt and pepper. Bake at 325° for 1½ hours.

BRAISED FENNEL

- 4 heads fennel
- 4 tbsp. unsalted butter sliced into pats
- 1 cup stock
- Salt and pepper
- ½ cup gruyere cheese, grated

Trim, core and cut in half the four fennel heads. Butter a baking dish and arrange the fennel in it. Add the pats of butter, stock, and salt and pepper and cover with buttered parchment paper. Cook in a preheated oven at 400° for 30 minutes. Remove the paper and baste the fennel, continue cooking for 10 to 20 minutes longer. The stock should have reduced somewhat. Now add the cheese and cook until it is melted and brown.

Venison Steak with Red Wine
Bittergreens and Cheese Salad
Garlic Toasts
Rhubarb Tart

Serves four

All game, because of its high protein content, continues to cook significantly after it has been removed from the heat source. But for some reason I have found it more so with venison than with other types of game. It is worth being aware of—you can always cook something more but not less. Also, not only does venison continue to cook, it then loses heat very quickly and becomes cold. I make an extra effort to serve venison on warmed plates or platters so it is still warm when it gets to the table.

VENISON STEAK WITH RED WINE

- 2 lbs. venison steak
- 2 tbsp. oil
- 6 tbsp. unsalted butter
- 2 tbsp. finely chopped shallots
- ⅔ cup good red wine (the better the wine, the better the sauce)
- ½ cup veal stock
- Salt and pepper

Pan fry the steak in oil until done. Remove to a platter. In the pan put one of the tablespoons of butter and the shallots over a medium heat and cook until they are just barely soft. Add the wine and bring to a boil and continue boiling until you have ⅓ left. Add the veal stock and simmer till half of that is left, you should have about ½ cup liquid in all now. Slice the meat against the grain. Whisk in the remaining butter to the sauce and any of the juices from the steak on the platter. Season with salt and pepper and serve the sauce over the steak.

BITTERGREENS AND CHEESE SALAD

    Escarole, chicory or arugula
    Bibb lettuce
4 strips of bacon
3 oz. blue cheese
    Vinaigrette

Wash and dry the lettuce and greens and break into bite-size pieces. Cut the bacon into 1-inch pieces and fry till medium done, not crisp. Cut the cheese into cubes. Combine the lettuce, bacon and cheese and toss with the vinaigrette. Serve.

GARLIC TOASTS

    1 loaf French bread
    8 heads of firm garlic
    5 tbsp. good green olive oil
       Salt and pepper

Cut the French bread into ½-inch slices and toast on a cookie sheet in a 300° oven making sure both sides are lightly browned.

Separate all the garlic cloves, peel and remove any green sprouts. Boil all the cloves in a couple quarts of cold, salted water for 5 minutes. Drain and repeat the boiling process three more times. The garlic cloves should be easily pierced with a fork. Purée the cloves with the olive oil in a food processor or blender or mash with a fork. Add salt and pepper to taste. Spread the garlic purée on the toast and run under the broiler to glaze. Serve.

RHUBARB TART

½ lb. pastry (yours or a sheet of Pepperidge Farm Puff Pastry)
3 lbs. rhubarb (preferably the young sticks)
¾ cup sugar, plus enough to sprinkle on the pastry
1 lemon, grated
Splash of vanilla or sherry
⅔ cup crème fraîche, or a mixture of sour cream and heavy cream
2 tbsp. confectioners' sugar
½ tsp. powdered cloves

Roll out the pastry into a buttered 9-inch tart or pastry dish and refrigerate for 1 hour.

With a knife peel the thin outer layer from each stick of rhubarb and slice very thinly. Put in a heavy saucepan with the granulated sugar. Cover and cook 15 minutes over a medium low heat. Then remove the lid and turn the heat up to evaporate all the juices. Stir constantly so it will not stick and burn. Once it has become the consistency of jam remove and let cool. Add the lemon rind and a few drops of the vanilla or sherry.

Prick the bottom of the refrigerated pastry shell with a fork and place foil tightly over the pastry. Fill with pie weights or beans and cook on the lower shell of a preheated oven at 425° for 8 minutes. Remove the foil and weights, prick the crust again, sprinkle with a little granulated sugar and return it to the oven for 5 more minutes or until the crust is caramelized. Remove it from the oven and carefully slide the crust onto a cake rack to cool.

Whip the cream and sour cream (or just the crème fraîche) together with the confectioners' sugar and clove. When it's thick, spread it over the bottom of the pastry shell. Then spread the rhubarb over the whipped cream mixture and serve within 30 minutes, otherwise the crust becomes soggy.

Venison Calzone
Sliced Tomatoes with Basil
Fried Sage Leaves
Poached Pears

Serves four

Deer are everywhere, it seems. I was particularly impressed with that fact after visiting friends in Connecticut. Ed was on a deer hunt and I had ventured off to a Ducks Unlimited dinner unescorted. Rather than make the trip back to Massachusetts the same evening I stayed the night with friends. In the morning the offer of a quick pass through their back woods in search of deer was made. The concept of potentially shooting a deer in Connecticut while I was on a morning stroll and with Ed in the Maine woods for a week trying to get his deer tickled my fancy. Dressed improperly in the cocktail party attire of the previous evening and allowing only an hour for the hunt (only in Connecticut could the attire or time limit even vaguely work for a deer hunt), I was amazed to get a glimpse at some 20 good-sized deer in the space of that hour. And we would have had our venison had it not been for some near-sighted shooting on the part of my companion.

As some 122,816,330 pounds of wild venison are brought to the tables in America annually, variety in recipes is mandatory. This recipe offers a good change of pace from venison loaf or burgers.

VENISON CALZONE

- 3 cups all-purpose flour
- 2¼ tsp. or 1 pkg. dry yeast
- 2 tbsp. oregano
- 1 cup ground venison
- 1 clove garlic
- Bacon fat
- 1 cup eggplant, cubed

1 tbsp. oil
½ cup slivered gruyere cheese
¼ cup chopped parsley
Salt and pepper

In a medium size bowl mix 1 cup of the flour with the yeast and add enough warm water (not hot water) to make a moist and cohesive ball. Fill the bowl with warm water so the ball is covered. Let sit 5 to 15 minutes until the ball pops to the surface. Meanwhile take the remaining amount of flour (this can be all white flour or a mixture such as ⅔ white and ⅓ whole wheat) and put it on top of the counter. Make a trench in the middle of the pile and add the salt. Reconstitute the oregano by pouring a little hot water in with it first and then add it to the flour trench. You will need to add more water, as much as a cup or so, fluffing it into the flour with your fingers. The mixture should be slightly cohesive but not wet as the yeast/flour ball will be quite wet. When the ball has risen to the surface of the water, scoop it out and set in the middle of your pile of flour. Knead the ball and the flour together and continue to knead for 8 minutes or so. Put the dough in an oiled or floured bowl with a towel over it and place in a warm spot to rise two hours or until doubled in bulk. Punch down and roll out into a 6-inch by 12-inch rectangle.

Now brown the venison in the bacon fat and sauté the eggplant in the oil. Put the burger, eggplant, and grated cheese in layers in the center of the dough and sprinkle with parsley, salt, and pepper. Then pull the sides of the dough up over the meat mixture and wrap tightly, pinching the seams. Flip over so the seam is on the bottom. Let rise again and bake in a preheated oven at 425° till done (about 35-40 minutes).

FRIED SAGE LEAVES

½ cup large sage leaves
2 tbsp. unsalted butter
Salt

Fry the sage leaves in butter until they're stiff but not browned. Remove with wooden tongs and season with salt.

POACHED PEARS

- 4 ripe pears
- Lemon juice
- 2 cups water
- 1⅓ cups sugar
- 1 vanilla bean, split

Peel the pears with a vegetable peeler and core from the bottom with a melon baller. Rub the peeled pears with lemon juice. In a saucepan combine water, a few drops of lemon juice, and sugar and bring it to a boil. Add the split vanilla bean and reduce the heat. Simmer for 5 minutes. Then add the pears and continue to simmer for about 10 minutes or until the pears are tender. Remove the pears from the syrup and stand upright on a plate in the refrigerator. The chilled pears can be served with crème anglaise, whipped cream, chocolate shavings, or a liqueur over it.

**Venison Chops with Basil Cream
Homemade Pasta with Parsley
Salad with Hazelnut Dressing
Brandied Apricots with Crème Anglaise**

Serves four

VENISON CHOPS WITH BASIL CREAM

- 1 pint heavy cream
- ½ tbsp. dried basil
- 4 venison chops
- 1 tbsp. oil
- 1 tbsp. unsalted butter
- Splash of veal stock or brandy to deglaze
- Salt and pepper

Reduce the cream. Pour the cream into a frying pan, bring to a slow boil and add the basil. Simmer until halved in quantity and thick. If it gets too thick add a little water and stir. Meanwhile cook the chops. Brush away any bone chips left from butchering and remove all fat from the venison. In a frying pan with the hot oil and butter, sauté the chops very quickly, 2 or 3 minutes per side. Remember venison continues to cook long after it comes off the heat. The chops should be pink. Remove the chops and in the pan add a tiny amount of stock or brandy and deglaze; then add the basil cream. Stir and season with salt and pepper and serve with the chops.

HOMEMADE PASTA WITH PARSLEY

    1½ cups semolina
    2 eggs
       All-purpose flour for dusting
       Salt
       Couple of drops of olive oil for the boiling water
    2 tbsp. unsalted butter, melted
    2 tbsp. finely chopped parsley

Make a mountain of the semolina on the counter-top and then make a crater in the mountain. Lightly beat the eggs together and pour into the crater. With a fork bring the semolina into the egg mixture slowly until all the semolina is moist, then form into two small balls. If the dough is at all sticky, add more semolina—the dough needs to be very dry. Knead for 10-20 minutes and then shape into two 8-inch-long (or so) snakes. Cut each snake into 6 pieces. Take one of the pieces and knead it for a few minutes. Flatten with the palm of your hand until it is thin enough to crank through the pasta machine on the thickest setting (#1 on the classic machine). Fold the pasta and crank through again. Repeat this two more times on this setting. Now put the pasta sheet through each progressive setting on the machine without folding it until the pasta sheet is the desired thickness. For me, this is usually after the second to the last setting (#5). Finally cut the pasta and lay on a floured cutting board and sprinkle with all-purpose flour. Toss pasta with your fingers so it is well dusted with the flour. Repeat the procedure for the remaining pieces of dough. The pasta may now be left to dry.

Of course dried pasta can be stored or cooked immediately. Freshly-made pasta cooks very quickly in boiling water—be sure to add salt to the water and a drop of oil—only about 2 to 3 minutes. Drain and toss with melted butter and parsley.

HAZELNUT SALAD

    Boston lettuce
½ cup toasted and crushed hazelnuts
¾ cup hazelnut oil
3 tbsp. vinegar
1 clove shallot, chopped fine
1 tsp. prepared mustard
    Salt and pepper

Wash and spin dry the lettuce. Toast the hazelnuts in the oven.

Remove and cover with a tea towel to steam. Rub the skins off the nuts and chop fine. Sprinkle over the lettuce.

Combine the remaining ingredients in the blender and zip on high for a few seconds. Pour over the salad and toss.

BRANDIED APRICOTS WITH CRÈME ANGLAISE

1 lb. apricots
3 cups brandy (or enough to cover)

Place the apricots in a jar and cover with brandy. Seal and let stand at least 48 hours. Serve with crème anglaise (see next page).

CRÈME ANGLAISE

4 yolks
Pinch of salt
¼ cup sugar
½ cup milk
½ cup cream
1 tbsp. liqueur (Grand Marnier is good) or vanilla

Whisk together the yolks, salt and sugar. Combine the milk and cream and whisk that into the yolks. Cook over a medium-high heat stirring constantly until it thickens quite suddenly. Remove from the heat, strain and then whisk till cool. Add the liqueur or vanilla and spoon the crème anglaise over the cooked apples. Can be served hot or cold.

Game Care

Ed brought home the first deer of our life together—to a Boston apartment. Our small daughter in my arms, we stood on the curb of the city street marveling over the beautiful animal lying across the top of the Jeep. Musing slightly over the incongruity of the situation, I watched as the car disappeared down the dark street bound for the suburban home of a friend where it was to be "hung." And the slow realization came over me: "What now?"

At that point I knew only to worry about the obvious mechanics of how to get a whole carcass into the form of cut-up pieces of meat. What I was to learn subsequently was that what had come before the car-top journey and then the processing of the meat was actually of equal significance and consequence to the quality of the various cuts of meat and how they should be cooked. And worry is what I would have done had I any game care experience back then. That deer had been through a lot by the time it got to Boston.

It was a particularly large whitetail, about 210 pounds field-dressed. Ed had shot it in a very remote area of New Hampshire and worked the better part of a day—along with his hunting companion Larry—just to drag the deer back to camp. But then there was an even greater challenge: the camp and the deer were on one side of a swollen stream and the car was on the other. Getting the deer across the stream and onto the roof of the car was going to be no easy task. The frail, skinny, rope bridge which dangled above the stream was meant only for a thin-framed human walking single-file and didn't seem the way to go. On the other hand, forging the waist-deep rocky-bottomed stream with the 210 pounds of dead weight seemed, at best, un-fun. Weighing the options carefully, the men struck on a third possibility, a somewhat modified rope and pulley system—or the old wrap around the tree trick—for accomplishing their task of getting the deer cartop.

With Larry on one side of the stream, he fixed a rope to the deer's antlers, and Ed walked the footbridge with the other end of the rope to wrap around a big tree on the opposite side of the stream. The rope could have been fastened securely around the tree, Larry gone to Ed's side of the river, and the two men could have hauled the beast together or even enlisted the muscle of the car. That could have been the way it worked, yes it could have been a plan. But in eager anticipation of Ed's end of the rope being secured, Larry dragged the deer very close, too close, to the stream's edge. Then, in a forceful flash, the stream snatched the carcass, and caused the premature launching of the deer. With the other end of the rope not yet fastened, the deer was afloat and gone! And without those antlers grabbing as it went, the deer would have been gone forever downstream. But the big deer's trophy rack snagged a semi-submerged log and brought Ed plunging mid-stream to wrestle with the antlers, the submerged log, and the current in order to save his great prize. Then there was trying to get the deer on top of the car, and driving it eight hours to Boston. Yes, a lot had happened to this deer and probably it wasn't good, at least in terms of its culinary value.

It was likely the day of being pulled through the woods, the stream-side bath, the cold, cold of the water and then the warmer air would not have enhanced the flavor or tenderness of the meat, or could it? While standing curb-side in that city street so long ago, I didn't know enough to care. But today I'd know to consider the trials and tribulations unique to that deer—or duck or pheasant or rabbit—and also to have some other questions for the hunter: Was it a clean shot? Had the critter run (or flown) far after being shot? How long and at what temperature had it lain dead before being field dressed? What was its probable diet and age? What a general pain in the neck I would have made of myself. But all those elements can in fact, or according to folk lore anyway, affect the meat.

What is fact and what is myth? Much has been written in game cookbooks and in the outdoor literature about how different elements, both in the field as well as in the kitchen, affect the taste of game. It always has been very hard for me to discern what is simply the opinion of the writer (or is included more for the sake of tradition) and what is based on fact. I wanted scientific reasons for why venison, partridge, pheasant should be hung—or do they in fact really need to be hung at all—and if so for how long, head up or down, etc. Fortunately, coming from a family of meat-packers and food technologists, I have some sources of scientific information.

My father is a chemical engineer who spent 35 years in the food industry specializing in food processing and meat packing in scores of countries around the world. Here is some of the information he provided about the care and treatment of meat.

About freezing:

Of course, the first consequence of freezing is that it cuts down on bacteria growth and allows us to keep the meat for a long time. At the same time it has several other consequences. Meat has a very high water content—over 65%. Freezing causes the globules of water cells to crystallize. The size of the crystals is in inverse proportion to the speed of freezing. If the freezing occurs quickly the crystals will be quite small. If the freezing happens slowly the crystals will be quite large and cause any yet-unfrozen water to exude out of the meat. In addition, as the temperature is lowered expansion of the water cells occurs and may cause a bursting of the cells if done slowly. Consequently, slow freezing can cause the meat to lose moisture and also become mushy. Slow thawing, as in a refrigerator, may have a similar effect. As the temperature of the refrigerator goes up and down the cells may crystallize and then liquify causing the same bursting and exuding of moisture. The blowers inside frost-free freezers, or any air movement, can cause freezer burn, a desiccation of the meat.

All that this suggests is that if meat is going to be frozen it should be done as quickly as possible, well wrapped and then thawed quickly (or at least at a consistently warm temperature). The suggested wrap for frozen meat is a first layer of aluminum foil to obtain rapid heat transfer and protection from air and then 12 hours later a second wrap of a plastic bag to protect further against air movement. Added tips are to press the foil tightly around the meat. Remember to label with weight, date, and to grade the piece and when the baggie goes over it to suck the air out before the twist-tie goes on. The labeling, of course, helps you know what you're cooking before you've thawed it. Nothing worse than to plan an *ooh la la* dinner and then discover you've thawed that messed-up stew meat that's been in the freezer a year (almost all meat has significantly deteriorated after a year of the freezer).

About smoking meat:

A hot smoking of meat, like freezing, has the effect of cutting down on the bacteria growth, allowing the meat to be kept longer. Smoking does three things to meat: it heats it, dries it and adds flavor to it. The long, slow heating process of smoking brings the temperature of the meat to above 127° or the "denaturing point." This changes the color of the meat from blood red and kills some, but not all, of the bacteria. The meat also becomes firmer. The drying cuts the moisture content and makes the meat less hospitable to bacteria, while the addition of the smoked flavor adds some acidity, making it even more difficult for certain bacteria to grow. The amount of time a piece of smoked meat can be kept depends largely on the effectiveness of the heating, drying and flavoring process. This may be difficult to determine. Often we don't know much about how well a piece of meat has been smoked or how long it's been hanging around since the smoking. The general guidelines are these: A commercially cured and smoked ham can be kept for up to a year in a cool, dry place; something you smoke yourself in the backyard can probably go as long as a month in the refrigerator and probably six months to a year in the freezer. Fortunately, meat is quite forgiving. And, as my father would say, "it will let you know when it's had it."

About hanging meat:

Hanging meat, or aging it, tenderizes it. The aging process begins after rigor mortis has peaked. Rigor mortis begins a few hours after the animal has been shot and increases very rapidly, peaking at about 10 to 24 hours. It then will decline with the curve flattening at about 48 hours and will continue to decline for two weeks. The meat will be at its toughest stage during rigor mortis and then it will become increasingly more tender. The amount of time for aging to occur is significantly affected by the air temperature. This is why the location of your hunt has a great deal to do with how long the meat should be hung and how it should be handled right after shooting it. In general, the higher the temperature the faster the aging process and the softer the meat. Of course, if the temperature is too high growth of bacteria is promoted, too. Consequently how long an animal should be hung has to do with your own taste buds and the temperature control over the period of aging (a good regulated temperature of 45-50 degrees is optimum).

Taste being the key, it is difficult to advise in such matters. But since much of what is found acceptable is based on what Americans are used to, the guideline for venison might start at what is desirable for beef, and in this country all beef is aged about two weeks.

We age our venison anywhere from a week to two, depending on the weather and how long the temperatures hold steady. This, of course, is the bottom line for us. If not rigged with a cooler, the length of time for aging becomes somewhat a function of what the weatherman dictates and has not much to do with what has been advised or found to be most desirable.

About cleaning the meat:

In our culture the taste of blood is generally not well received and some lengths should be gone to clean the game properly if you wish to comply with cultural norms. Of course, the hunter can always help by trying for a lung shot on the bigger animals such as a deer. The lung shot will guarantee the least amount of damage, blood or otherwise, to the meat, and also kill the animal quickly. Hanging the animal for aging or butchering with the head to the ground is suggested for cleanliness sake. A spraying with water before freezing or refrigeration is also advisable for meat in order to keep down the bacteria count. Use paper towel to pat the meat dry rather than the kitchen dish towel (no need to add the bacteria from the towel back into the meat).

Other things which can affect the flavor of the meat:

Age, size and even sex of the animal can affect the taste. This is especially true of the glandular meat (neck and shoulder meat) in deer. An old, big female is likely to have tougher, stronger flavored neck meat than the saddle from a young, small buck.

The flavor of whatever the critter has been eating is most intense in the fat and will flavor the meat if left on while cooking. To soak meat in water, salted water, or milk causes some exuding of flavor from the meat. Then, after the exuding, the flavor of the salt and milk will mask what the animal has been feeding on.

The effect of cooking:

The purpose of cooking a piece of meat is to render it more digestible and to eliminate any diseases. The specifics of how something is cooked get into a matter of taste, of course, but certain generalizations can be made. The longer and slower meat is cooked the more tender and easily digestible it becomes (it also loses more of the vitamins). The higher and shorter the heat, the juicier the meat.

So how do you positively anticipate correctly the taste of your venison? In short, you can't. You can know that a neck roast from a big, old, bark-eating female deer with blood and fat all over it and cooked ten hours after it was shot or a year after being in the freezer, unwrapped, then cooked on a high heat for a long time will taste like shoe leather. But hopefully you knew that before you read this. Every time an element is altered, the taste is altered. And what must be kept in perspective are those elements which you have some control over. Hopefully the generalized facts listed above which determine flavor and texture will help you determine what things you are going to strive to control. It is possible to control the temperature for hanging by purchasing your very own $10,000 meat locker. It is possible to break the law and shoot a springtime buck. It is possible to eat only the saddle roast from a deer dead one hour. All these things are possible, but often impractical or illegal or un-fun. Focus on what suits you to control and beware of the risks when you do cut corners. Certainly the height of control is to make the meat into what we eat every day: created, maintained, slaughtered and packaged meat with a predictable flavor. Hopefully the adventurous spirit in you is willing to try to eat and cook what the hunter presents. Be smart and energetic when preserving and cooking game, but also willing to improvise when a lack of ideal circumstances dictates it.

Lastly, remember that in the final analysis what often constitutes proper game care is usually linked to what makes the meat taste "good." And what constitutes "good" in taste is not always agreed upon.

Index

Apricots, Brandied, 86

Baby Spinach and Arugula Salad with Avocado and Egg, 16
Basil Bread, 42, 44
Beans
  Green, 50, 56
  Green and Beet Salad, 58
  White, puree, 70
Bibb Lettuce and Tomato Salad, 69
Bittergreens and Cheese Salad, 74, 76
Blue Cheese Polenta, 60, 61
Braised Fennel, 26, 29, 71, 73
Brandied Apricots with Crème Anglaise, 84, 86
Bread
  Basil, 44
  Fennel Seed, 18
  Fried, 22, 24
  Pepperoni, 54
Butterscotch, Homemade, 68

Cake
  Crusted Blueberry and Cream, 40
Calzone, Venison, 80
Child, Julia, 13
Chili, Venison Black Bean, 16
Clafoutis, 26, 30
Coffee Granita, 56, 59

Coffee Ice Cream with Hazelnut Liqueur, 69
Crème Anglaise, 83, 84, 86
Crisps, Ginger Angel, 21
Crusted Blueberry and Cream Cake, 37, 40
Custard Oranges, 42, 46

Fennel Seed Bread, 18
Fennel, braised, 29
Fresh Figs, 71
Fresh Fruit, 22
Fried Bread, 22, 24
Fried Potato Skins, 31, 33
Fried Sage Leaves, 80, 82

Game Care, 89
  cleaning, 94
  effect of cooking, 94
  freezing, 91
  hanging, 93
  other factors, 94
  smoking, 92
Garlic Toasts, 74, 77
Ginger Angel Crisps, 16, 21
Gray's Sporting Journal, 11, 60
Green Beans, 50, 56, 58
Green Beans and Beet Salad, 56, 58
Green Salad, 42, 53
Grilled Red Pepper Salad, 31, 34, 63

Grilled Venison Steak with Rosemary Butter, 69

Hazelnut liqueur, 69
Hazelnut Salad, 86
Homemade Pasta with Parsley, 84, 85

Ice Cream, 35
  strawberry, 35
  vanilla with homemade butterscotch sauce, 63

Lacey Act, 13, 14

Mashed Potatoes with Fresh Basil, 63, 65
Meyer Lemon Sherbet, 47, 49

Oranges
  custard, 46
  stuffed, 53, 55

Pasta, homemade, 37, 39, 84, 85
  with parsley, 85
Pears, Poached, 83
Pepperoni Bread, 53, 54
Persillade Potatoes, 50, 51
Poached Pears, 80, 83
Polenta
  blue cheese, 61
Potato skins, fried, 33
Potatoes
  and Porcini, 26, 28
  Mashed with fresh basil, 65
  Persillade, 51
  Roast with Rosemary, 57

Rhubarb Tart, 74, 78

Roast Potatoes, 47, 56, 57
Roast Potatoes with Rosemary, 56, 57

Saddle of Venison, 26, 27, 47
Sage Leaves, Fried, 82
Salad, 22
  grilled red pepper, 34
  Hazelnut, 86
  vegetable, 25
  with Hazelnut Dressing, 84
Sautéed Watercress, 47, 48
Sherbet, Meyer Lemon, 49
Spinach and Bibb Lettuce Salad, 60
Stock, Veal, 66
Strawberry Ice, 31, 35, 60, 62
Strawberry Ice Cream, 31, 35
Stuffed Oranges, 53, 55
Sweet Potato Gratin, 71, 72

Tart
  Rhubarb, 78
Tarte Tatin, 50, 52
Toasts, Garlic, 77
Tomatoes
  Sliced with Basil, 80
  Sun-dried, 43

Vanilla Ice Cream with Homemade Butterscotch Sauce, 63
Vegetable Salad, 22, 25
Venison
  Black Bean Chili, 16
  Burgers with Chateaubriand Butter, 22
  Calzone, 80
  Chops with Basil Cream, 84

Chops with Blue Cheese and Caraway Seeds, 71
Chops with Mustard Butter, 56
Chops with Pignolis and Red Peppers, 53
Grilled with Rosemary Butter, 69
in Europe, 13
in New Zealand, 13
Native Americans and, 12
Saddle of, 26
Scallops, 50
Steak with Red Wine, 74
Steak with Wild Mushrooms, 60
Steaks Marinated, 63
Stew, 37
Stew with Artichoke Hearts and Sun-dried Tomatoes, 42
Strip Steaks, 31
wild and farm-raised deer, differences between , 14
with Port, 47
Venison Burgers with Chateaubriand Butter, 22, 23
Venison Calzone, 80
Venison Chops with Basil Cream, 84
Venison Chops with Blue Cheese and Caraway Seeds, 71
Venison Chops with Mustard Butter, 56
Venison Chops with Pignolis and Red Peppers, 53
Venison Scallops, 50

Venison Steak with Red Wine, 74, 75
Venison Steak with Wild Mushrooms, 60
Venison Steaks Marinated, 63, 64
Venison Stew, 37, 38, 42, 43
Venison Stew with Artichoke Hearts and Sun-dried Tomatoes, 42, 43
Venison Strip Steaks, 31, 32
Venison with Port, 47

W atercress, 48
Waters, Alice, 13
White Bean Purée, 69, 70

About the author:

REBECCA GRAY has written eleven books about food, including the best-selling *Eat Like a Wild Man*. She has been a contributing editor for *Sports Afield* and *Attaché* and written for *Field & Stream*, *SAVEUR*, *Town & Country*, *Playboy*, *Outside*, *Martha Stewart Living*, and many other publications. Most recently she served as an expert editor for the 75th anniversary edition of the *Joy of Cooking*. With her husband, Ed Gray, she founded *Gray's Sporting Journal*, the prestigious magazine about hunting and fishing. She lives in Lyme, New Hampshire.

www.ingramcontent.com/pod-product-compliance
Lightning Source LLC
Chambersburg PA
CBHW022213090526
44584CB00013BA/839